Dinosaurs Alive!

Velociraptor

and other speedy killers

Jinny Johnson

Illustrated by Graham Rosewarne

W

FRANKLIN WATTS
LONDON•SYDNEY

An Appleseed Editions book

First published in 2007 by Franklin Watts

Franklin Watts
338 Euston Road, London NW1 3BH

Franklin Watts Australia
Level 17/207 Kent St, Sydney, NSW 2000

© 2007 Appleseed Editions

Created by Appleseed Editions Ltd,
Well House, Friars Hill, Guestling,
East Sussex TN35 4ET

Designed by Helen James
Edited by Mary-Jane Wilkins
Artwork by Graham Rosewarne

ISBN 978 07496 7543 1

Dewey Classification: 567.912

A CIP catalogue for this book is available from the British Library

Photograph on page 29 by Sally A.Morgan; Ecoscene/CORBIS

Printed in China

Franklin Watts is a division of Hachette Children's Books

Contents

Dinosaurs' world

A dinosaur was a kind of reptile that lived millions of years ago. Dinosaurs lived long before there were people on Earth.

We know about dinosaurs because many of their bones and teeth have been discovered. Scientists called palaeontologists (pay-lee-on-tol-ojists) learn a lot about the animals by studying these bones.

The first dinosaurs lived about 225 million years ago. They disappeared – became extinct – about 65 million years ago.

Some scientists believe that birds are a type of dinosaur, so they say there are still dinosaurs living all around us!

Ornithomimus

TRIASSIC
248 to 205 million years ago
Some dinosaurs that lived at this time:
Coelophysis, Eoraptor, Liliensternus,
Plateosaurus, Riojasaurus, Saltopus

EARLY JURASSIC
205 to 180 million years ago
Some dinosaurs that lived at this time:
Crylophosaurus, Dilophosaurus, Lesothosaurus,
Massospondylus, Scelidosaurus, Scutellosaurus

Lesothosaurus

LATE JURASSIC
180 to 144 million years ago
Some dinosaurs that lived at this time:
Allosaurus, Apatosaurus, Brachiosaurus,
Ornitholestes, Stegosaurus, Yangchuanosaurus

EARLY CRETACEOUS
144 to 98 million years ago
Some dinosaurs that lived at this time:
Baryonyx, Giganotosaurus, Iguanodon, Leaellynasaura,
Muttaburrasaurus, Nodosaurus, Sauropelta

LATE CRETACEOUS
98 to 65 million years ago
Some dinosaurs that lived at this time:
Ankylosaurus, Gallimimus, Maiasaura, Triceratops,
Tyrannosaurus, Velociraptor

Tyrannosaurus

Velociraptor

Not all meat-eating dinosaurs were giants. Velociraptor was only about the size of a large dog, but it was still a very fierce predator.

This dinosaur could run fast, standing upright on its slender legs. It may have hunted in packs.

Velociraptor is well-known because it had a starring role in the *Jurassic Park* films. But the dinosaurs in the film were much larger than the real-life Velociraptor.

The dinosaur was probably covered with feathers rather than scales, but it could not fly.

This is how you say
Velociraptor:
Vel-oss-ee-rap-tor

Velociraptor was a very agile dinosaur. It could leap on its prey and attack it with sharp claws.

VELOCIRAPTOR

Group: theropods (Dromaeosaurs)

Length: up to 1.8 metres

Lived in: Mongolia

When: Late Cretaceous, 84-80 million years ago

Inside Velociraptor

Velociraptor might have been small,
but it was strong and well equipped
for hunting.

This predator had powerful jaws lined with
about 80 teeth. They had jagged edges for
attacking prey and eating meat.

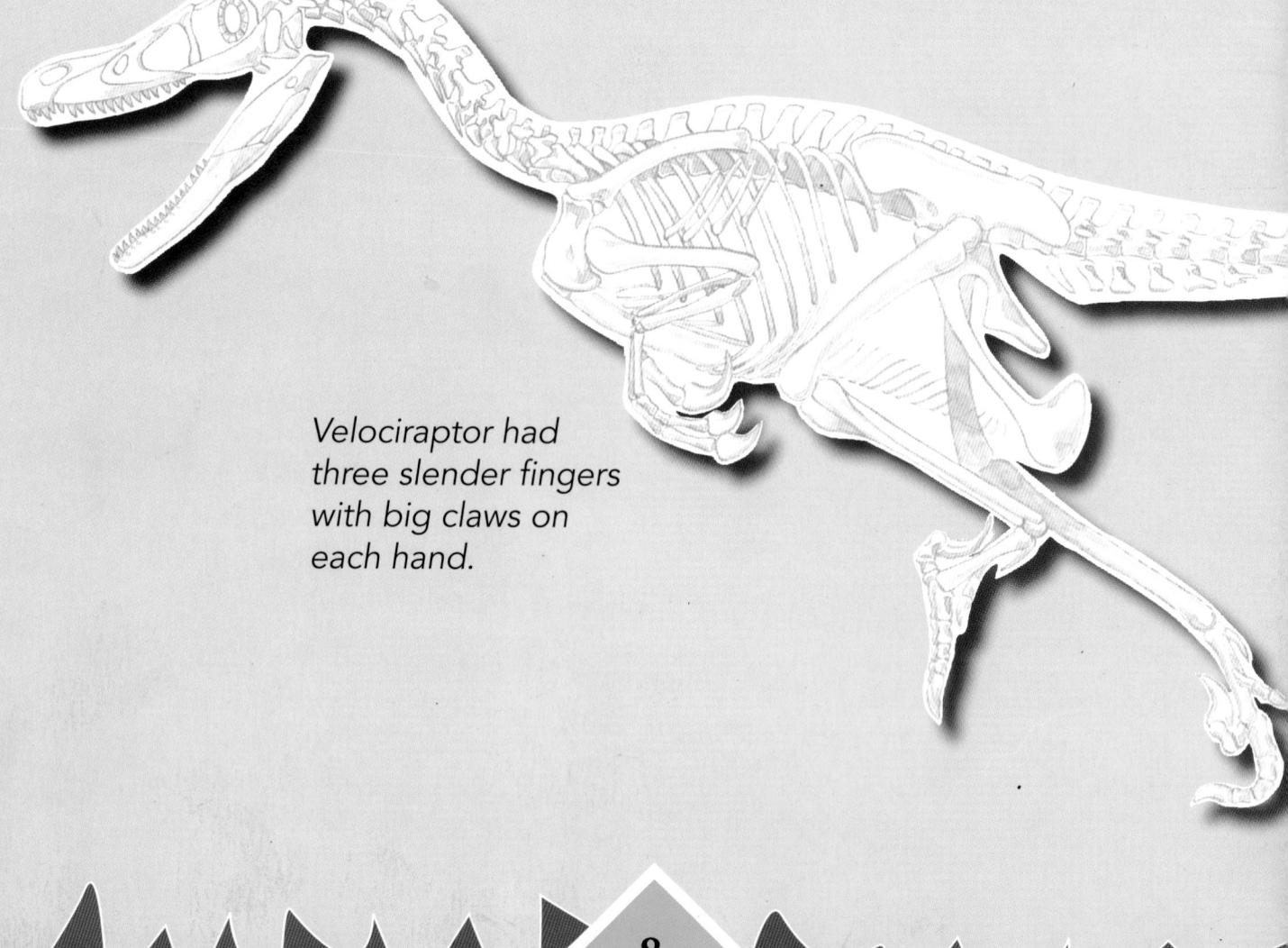

*Velociraptor had
three slender fingers
with big claws on
each hand.*

Each foot had four toes, one with a large, curved claw twice the size of the rest. The dinosaur held this claw off the ground when it was running so that it stayed sharp.

The many bones in Velociraptor's long tail helped to strengthen it. This dinosaur held its tail straight out like a rod to help it balance as it ran.

Dinosaurs lived long before there were people on Earth. But here you can see how big this dinosaur was compared with a seven-year-old child.

Velociraptor in action

A pack of Velociraptors hunting together could bring down animals much larger than themselves.

Experts once thought that Velociraptor slashed at the flesh of its prey with its claws. They now believe that the dinosaur killed by piercing the neck of its prey with a sharp claw.

Some fossils found in Mongolia showed a Velociraptor battling with a Protoceratops (pro-toe-serra-tops) dinosaur. The left claw of the Velociraptor was plunged into the neck of the other dinosaur. The two probably died together in a sandstorm that blew up as they fought.

Even fierce hunters like Velociraptor didn't always win their battles. Protoceratops had a heavy, bony neck frill to protect it. It defended itself with its sharp beak.

Deinonychus and Dromaeosaurus

These two dinosaurs were relatives of Velociraptor. They, too, were fast moving hunters which could speed along on their strong back legs at 60 kilometres an hour.

This is how you say Dromaeosaurus:
Drom-ee-oh-sore-us

DROMAEOSAURUS

Group: theropods (Dromaeosaurs)

Length: up to 1.8 metres

Lived in: North America

When: Late Cretaceous, 76-74 million years ago

Both these dinosaurs had light, strong bodies. They could leap on their prey and move quickly to dodge lashing tails or horns.

12

Fossilized skulls show that these dinosaurs had large brains for their size. They had good hearing, sharp eyes and a strong sense of smell. These senses helped them to be good hunters.

DEINONYCHUS

Group: theropods (Dromaeosaurs)

Length: up to 3 metres

Lived in: North America

When: Early Cretaceous, 120-110 million years ago

This is how you say Deinonychus: Die-non-eye-kus

Compsognathus

Speedy little Compsognathus was one of the smallest dinosaurs. It was only about the size of a large chicken, although it had a long tail.

Compsognathus moved upright on its long, slender back legs. It could run and jump to escape from predators, as well as to capture prey. It was a good hunter and preyed on small creatures such as lizards.

The name Compsognathus means 'elegant jaw' and the dinosaur's long jaws were lined with many small, sharp teeth. The dinosaur also had clawed fingers on each hand.

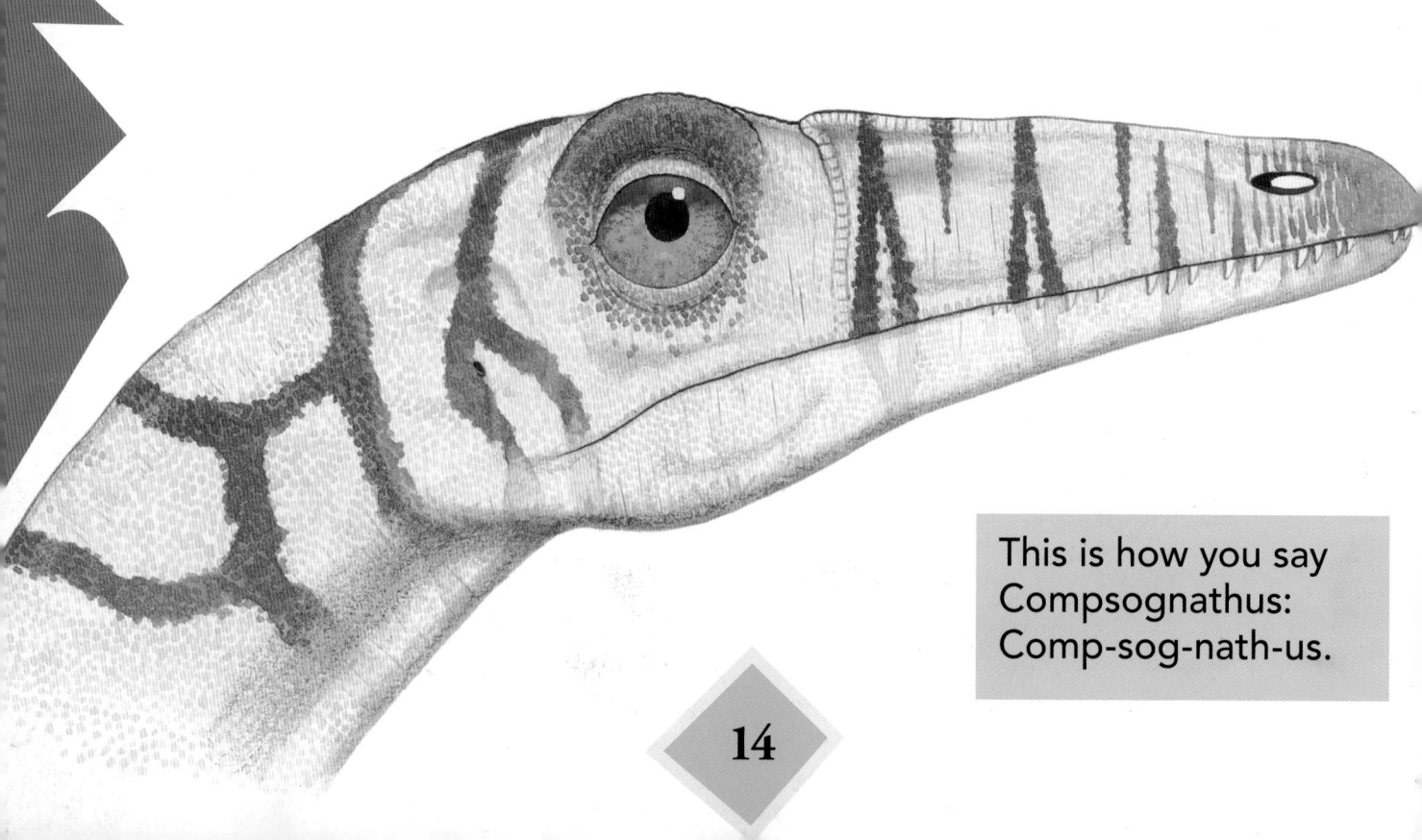

This is how you say Compsognathus: Comp-sog-nath-us.

The remains of lizards have been found inside the stomachs of some Compsognathus fossils.

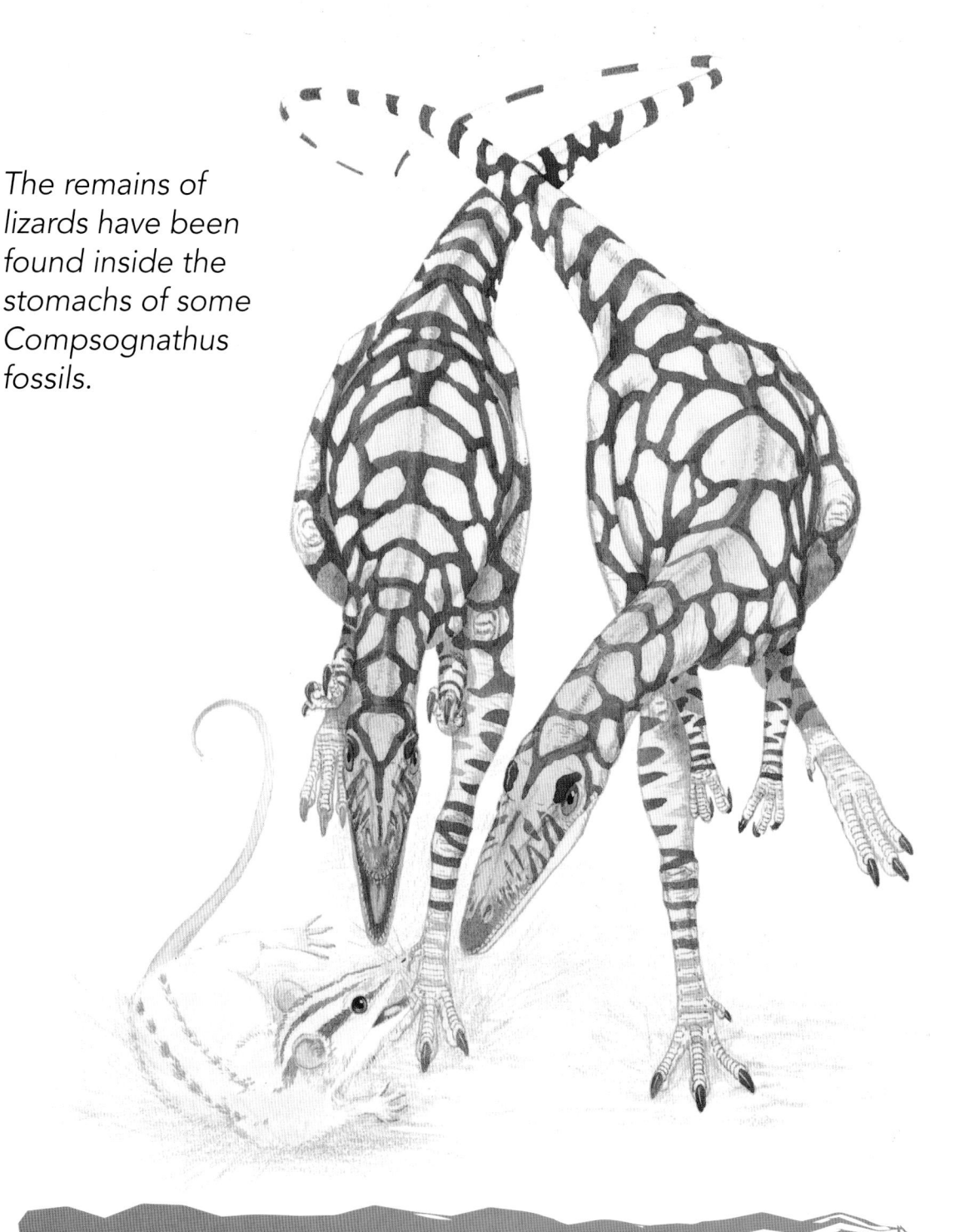

COMPSOGNATHUS

Group: theropods (Coelurosaurs)

Length: up to 65 centimetres

Lived in: Europe

When: Late Jurassic, 145-140 million years ago

Coelophysis

Coelophysis was one of the earliest meat-eating dinosaurs. Its name means 'hollow form' and it was given this name because its bones were partly hollow.

The hollow bones made Coelophysis very light, so it could run and jump as it hunted prey such as lizards, frogs, insects and fish.

Lots of Coelophysis fossils were found together in New Mexico 60 years ago. Experts think that they probably hunted in packs so they could attack larger animals.

Some of the fossils seemed to contain the bones of smaller Coelophysis. But scientists don't think the adults ate the young. They may have died together in a flood or storm.

COELOPHYSIS

Group: theropods (Coelurosaurs)

Length: up to 3 metres

Lived in: North America

When: Late Triassic, 225-220 million years ago

This is how you say Coelophysis:
See-low-fie-sis

Coelophysis raced around on slender back legs, seizing prey in its narrow toothed jaws. It had short arms and three-fingered clawed hands.

Gallimimus

The name Gallimimus means 'chicken mimic'. But Gallimimus was twice the size of an ostrich which meant it was much bigger than a chicken!

This lightly-built dinosaur ran fast on its slender back legs and was an intelligent, sharp-eyed hunter.

Gallimimus had claws on its hands and feet, which it used to seize prey such as lizards and insects. It probably ate the eggs of other dinosaurs as well as some fruit and leaves.

This is how you say Gallimimus:
Ga-lee-mee-mus

Gallimimus had no teeth in its beak-like jaws, so it swallowed food whole.

GALLIMIMUS

Group: theropods
(Ornithomimids)

Length: up to 6 metres

Lived in: Asia

When: Late Cretaceous,
74-70 million years ago

Gallimimus was speedy enough to catch fast-moving prey such as lizards.

Struthiomimus and Ornithomimus

Both these dinosaurs were fast-moving hunters like Gallimimus. They didn't have sharp teeth or massive claws so had to run fast to escape from predators.

STRUTHIOMIMUS

Group: theropods (Ornithomimids)

Length: up to 4 metres

Lived in: North America

When: Late Cretaceous, 76-74 million years ago

This is how you say Struthiomimus:
Struth-ee-oh-mee-mus

These dinosaurs could probably run at nearly 70 kilometres an hour. That's much faster than the speediest human runners.

Both dinosaurs held out their tails behind them to balance the weight at the front of the body.

They had large eyes to help them spot danger as well as prey. Their main food was probably small creatures, such as lizards and insects, but they may have eaten leaves and fruits as well.

ORNITHOMIMUS

Group: theropods (Ornithomimids)

Length: up to 4 metres

Lived in: North America

When: Late Cretaceous, 76-74 million years ago

This is how you say Ornithomimus:
Orn-ith-oh-mee-mus

Oviraptor

Long-legged Oviraptor was a fast dinosaur.
It probably ate small animals,
some plants and eggs.

Oviraptor had no teeth, but it did have very powerful jaws. These were shaped like a beak with sharp edges, so it could eat most types of food.

Oviraptor's name means 'egg thief', but the dinosaur doesn't deserve this name.

The first fossils of Oviraptor were found with a clutch of eggs, so it looked as though the dinosaur had been robbing another dinosaur's nest. But other fossils show that Oviraptor did not steal eggs, just protected its own.

OVIRAPTOR

Group: theropods (Oviraptorids)

Length: up to 2 metres

Lived in: Asia

When: Late Cretaceous, 85-75 million years ago

This is how you say Oviraptor:
Oh-vee-rap-tor

Oviraptor laid its eggs in a little hollow in the ground and probably sat on them to keep them warm and safe. The eggs had hard shells just like a bird's egg.

Bambiraptor

A 14-year-old boy found the bones
of this dinosaur when he was fossil hunting
in Montana in the United States.

The dinosaur turned out to be a new
kind and it was named Bambiraptor
because of its small size.

*This little creature was an agile
hunter. It ran fast after its prey
and held it in clawed fingers
while it delivered a killing bite.*

BAMBIRAPTOR

Group: theropods (Dromaeosaurs)

Length: up to 1 metre

Lived in: North America

When: Late Cretaceous, 84-71 million years ago

This is how you say Bambiraptor:
Bam-be-rap-tor.

Bambiraptor looked very like a bird.
It had light, hollow bones and may have
been covered with feathers.

The dinosaur ate lizards and small mammals.
It had large claws on the second toe of each
foot which helped it kill prey.

25

Caudipteryx

This bird-like dinosaur was about the size of a turkey, with long legs, short arms and a short tail.

Caudipteryx was covered with feathers which could be 20 centimetres long. The way the feathers lay on the body shows that the dinosaur could not fly. It also had a fan of tail feathers.

This is how you say Caudipteryx:
Caw-dip-ter-iks

CAUDIPTERYX

Group: theropods (Caudipterygid)

Length: up to 1 metre

Lived in: China

When: Early Cretaceous, 125-122 million years ago

26

Caudipteryx had a small head with a beak and long sharp teeth in its upper jaw.

The dinosaur may have swallowed stones to help grind up the food inside its body, as crocodiles and some birds do today.

Some experts think the feathers kept Caudipteryx warm. Others believe the dinosaur may have used its feathers to attract mates, as some birds do today.

Dinosaurs and birds

Did you know that the birds hopping round your garden are related to fierce meat-eating dinosaurs? That's what most scientists believe now.

Some experts have thought this for a while, but their ideas were hard to prove. Then fossils of some special dinosaurs were found in China in 1997.

The fossils were of dinosaurs which had feathers. They didn't have proper wings so couldn't fly, but their feathery coats would have kept them warm and may have helped them attract mates.

The feathered dinosaurs, such as Caudipteryx, looked very like Deinonychus and other fast-moving, hunting dinosaurs. They proved that birds and some types of dinosaurs are very closely linked.

Experts now think that other meat-eating dinosaurs, such as Deinonychus and Struthiomimus, may have had feathers too.

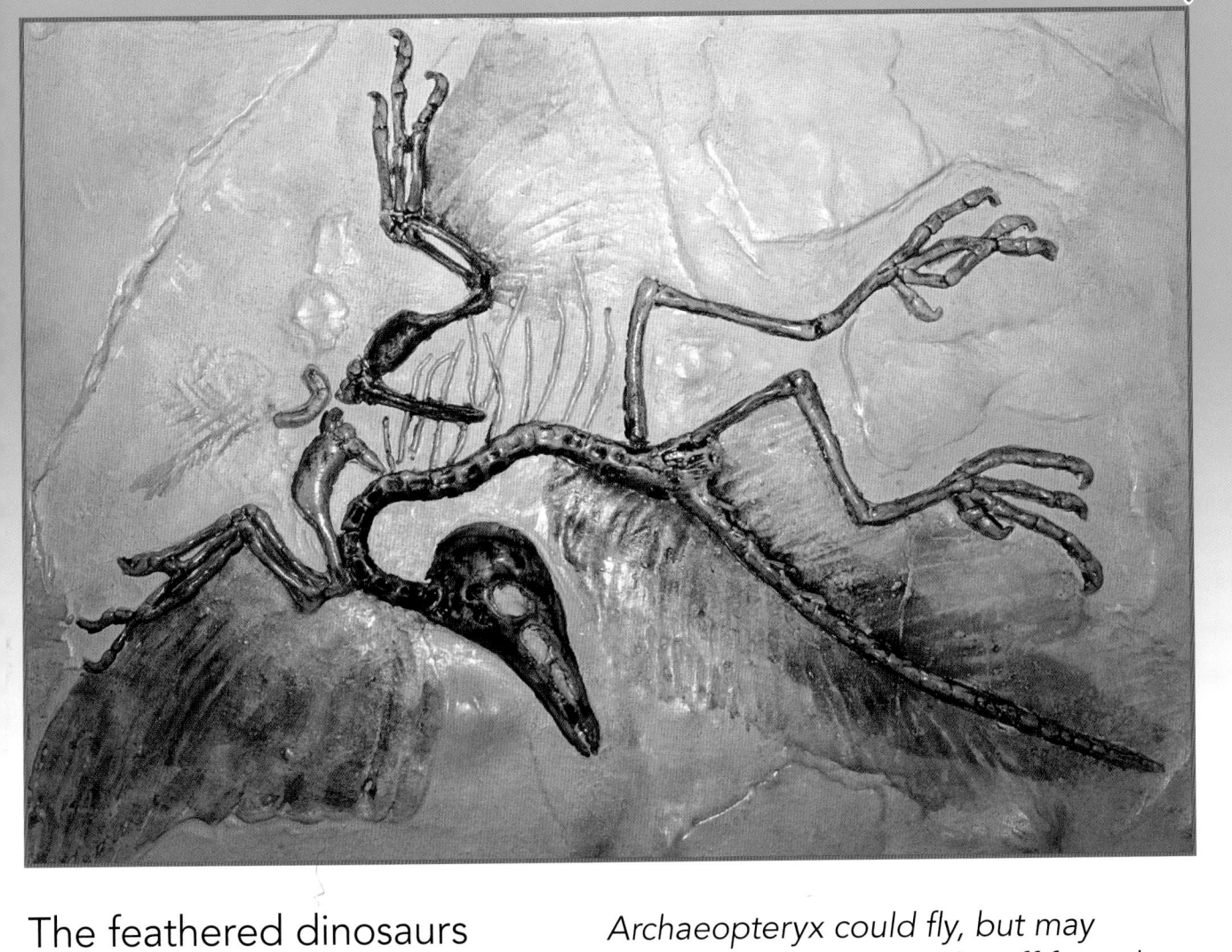

The feathered dinosaurs also looked very like the fossils of the first known bird – Archaeopteryx (ark-ee-op-ter-ix).

These fossils show a creature about the size of a magpie. It had feathers like a bird, but teeth and clawed fingers like a dinosaur. The fossils were found in Germany in 1861.

Archaeopteryx could fly, but may have found it hard to take off from the ground. It probably launched itself into the air from a tree. This picture shows one of the fossils found in Germany.

Words to remember

Cretaceous
The period of time from 144 to 65 million years ago.

fossils
Parts of an animal such as bones and teeth that
have been preserved in rock over millions of years.

horned dinosaur
Dinosaurs with big pointed horns on the head and
a sheet of bone called a frill at the back of the head.
Protoceratops was a horned dinosaur.

Jurassic
The period of time from 205 to 144 million years ago.

neck frill
The sheet of bone at the back of a horned dinosaur's head.

pack
Group of animals that ran around and hunted together.

palaeontologist
A scientist who looks for and studies fossils to find
out more about the creatures of the past.

predator
An animal that lives by hunting and killing
other animals.

prey
Animals caught and killed by hunters like Velociraptor.

reptile
An animal with a backbone and a dry scaly body.
Most reptiles lay eggs with leathery shells.
Dinosaurs were reptiles. Today's reptiles
include lizards, snakes and crocodiles.

scales
Covering on the body of a reptile. Scales are
made from keratin, like our fingernails.

skull
The bony framework of an animal's head.

Triassic
The period of time from 248 to 205 million years
ago. The first dinosaurs lived in the Triassic.

Index